IMAGES
of America

GOING-TO-THE-SUN
ROAD

This long, snow-covered straight stretch of the Going-to-the-Sun Road in the upper McDonald Valley is shown as it typically appears in April during the annual opening of the road. (Courtesy National Park Service.)

ON THE COVER: In 1933, National Park Service photographer George Alexander Grant paused at the Going-to-the-Sun Road's Big Bend (Mile 30) to photograph a fellow traveler admiring the huge, iconic snowbank that forms here annually. (Courtesy National Park Service.)

IMAGES
of America

GOING-TO-THE-SUN ROAD

Bill Yenne

ARCADIA
PUBLISHING

Copyright © 2013 by Bill Yenne
ISBN 978-0-7385-9698-3

Published by Arcadia Publishing
Charleston, South Carolina

Printed in the United States of America

Library of Congress Control Number: 2012943203

For all general information, please contact Arcadia Publishing:
Telephone 843-853-2070
Fax 843-853-0044
E-mail sales@arcadiapublishing.com
For customer service and orders:
Toll-Free 1-888-313-2665

Visit us on the Internet at www.arcadiapublishing.com

The author (left) and Bill Dakin pause along the Going-to-the-Sun Road near Mile 33, just east of the Big Drift area and a few hundred feet west of the East Side Tunnel. Clements Mountain (8,760 feet) forms the backdrop. (Author's collection.)

CONTENTS

ACKNOWLEDGMENTS

In writing a factual narrative about places that are familiar from our earliest memories, we recall our own experiences, as well as stories that were told by those who were there before us and who contribute to what we know and how we feel about a place.

Leona Harrington was my third- and fourth-grade teacher at the three-room West Glacier School. Her memories of Apgar and the West Side went back to 1914 and a personal acquaintance with the earliest pioneers.

My father also told stories during the nearly two decades that we lived inside Glacier National Park at Park Headquarters, a quarter mile off the Going-to-the-Sun Road. He was born and raised near the park and attended campfire sessions at Lake McDonald, presided over by Charley Russell when Glacier Park was new. He started work in Glacier in 1932 and spent most of his National Park Service career there, through his retirement in 1969, and continued to work for concessionaires on government special projects in the park for another 20 years. During the 1950s and 1960s, as I was growing up at Park Headquarters, he was Glacier's backcountry trails supervisor; he became supervisor of roads in the later decade.

Bill Dakin, a high school classmate, went on to work in Glacier in 1973 and worked on the Going-to-the-Sun Road for a dozen years from 1976 to 1988. A crew foreman for West Side roads, he is most singularly notable for having been an official speaker at the podium for the commemoration of both the 50th anniversary of the road in 1983 and the 75th in 2008. My most fondly remembered trip across the entire length of the Going-to-the-Sun Road in this century is the round trip that I took with Bill a few years ago. The road can be driven in two hours, but it took us all day, because we had to stop so often to look at stuff and go off on tangents—tall tales and recalled experiences.

Our memories, our experiences, and the experiences distilled from others comprise the spirit that underlies the narrative of this book.

INTRODUCTION

The Going-to-the-Sun Road is rightfully recognized as one of the most spectacular alpine highways in the world. Since its formal dedication in 1933, it has been the centerpiece of the visitor experience in Glacier National Park. The vast majority of park visitors drive its 51 miles, and none but the most jaded leave without being impressed or amazed. More than a few find themselves unnerved by the steepness, and many pause to marvel with astonishment at the work of the original engineers and builders.

The landscape is one of peerless beauty, but the road itself is an engineering masterpiece. The road has been in the National Register of Historic Places since 1985 and has also been a National Historic Landmark (NHL) since 1997.

A seasonal road, most of it is generally closed between mid-September and early June because of heavy snow, although it occasionally opens in May. The latest openings to date since its July 15, 1933, dedication have been July 2, 2008, July 10, 1943, and July 13, 2011. The earliest opening was on May 16, 1987.

It was in 1910, thanks to the efforts of people such as James J. Hill of the Great Northern Railway and the great naturalist George Bird Grinnell that a million acres of Northwestern Montana were set aside and officially designated as Glacier National Park. Indeed, Grinnell had described the place as "the Crown of the Continent," a description which is borne our by all who drive the Going-to-the-Sun Road.

George C. "Doc" Ruhle, who was park naturalist in Glacier from 1929 to 1941 and who is officially credited with naming the road, wrote in his 1949 *Guide to Glacier* that:

> The Going-to-the-Sun Highway [as it was known in the early days] is universally proclaimed as one of the great highways of the world. It skirts the shores of beautiful lakes, winds through deep cedar forests carpeted with ferns, passes lofty waterfalls and foaming cataracts, half-tunnels lofty cliffs, climbs gently but steadily above timber line to the meadows of alpine flowers on Logan Pass. It clings precariously to the Garden Wall, out of which it is hewn, yet is wide and safe with a strong protective guard-rail of stone constructed for miles along it. When it is opened for travel in June, it runs through canyons of snow a dozen or more feet deep, and a thousand crystal waterfalls cascade upon it.

The reckoning of its length varies from 53 miles (counting sections outside the park connecting it to US Highway 2 on the West Side and US Highway 89 on the East Side) to 48.7 miles on the NHL documents, which measures it from the foot of Lake McDonald. In this book, my reckoning is based on the 51 miles within Glacier National Park boundaries.

The idea for the road goes back to plans for visitor access, envisioned when the park was created. At the time that Glacier became a national park, a scant handful of trails reached into this wilderness wonderland of snowcapped peaks and crystal-clear lakes. A two-mile wagon road had been built by Dimon Apgar between the Great Northern Railway station at Belton and the foot of Lake McDonald, where he and others had homesteaded around the 1890s. This road was substantially upgraded under park superintendent William Logan in 1911. Plans were made for roads along the shores of Lake McDonald, but the National Park Service had little money, so road construction was in the hands of entrepreneurs.

In 1909, John Lewis had acquired a rustic lodge 10 miles up on the east shore of Lake McDonald, which had been built in 1896 by George Snyder. In turn, he replaced it with a much grander hotel (still in use) in 1914. Because access to the property was by boat from the foot of the lake, and the government was slow to act, Lewis undertook construction of a road to his hotel on his own initiative. This was completed in 1922.

During the park's first decade, while Lewis worked on the Lake McDonald Road on the West Side of the park, the Great Northern Railway, under Louis Hill, the son of the founder, undertook an extensive building program of their own on the East Side. The Great Northern built a grand Glacier Park Lodge across from their station at Midvale (now East Glacier), and more than 50 miles of road (now part of US 89) paralleling the park's eastern boundary from Midvale northward. From this, they built a series of spur roads extending a few miles into the park, and at the end of each, they built a rustic accommodations. These included the chalets at Two Medicine Lake, Cut Bank Creek, and St. Mary Lake. At the end of the northernmost spur road, they constructed the Many Glacier Hotel. Still is use today, it was for many years the largest hotel in Montana.

Meanwhile, the National Park Service began considering a variety of ideas for a "Transmountain Road" to connect the East and West Sides of Glacier National Park, providing automobile access to the spectacular scenery of the park interior. As National Park Service landscape engineer Thomas Vint noted in a 1925 memo, the route should "lie lightly on the landscape," allowing motorists to experience the magnificence of the natural beauty of the park with minimal impact on the environment.

One

PLANNING THE ROAD

From the confluence of McDonald Creek and Logan Creek (originally Trapper Creek), various options were considered for crossing the Continental Divide at the crest of the Lewis Range of the Rocky Mountains. T. Warren Allen of the office of public roads, who had planned roads in Yosemite and Sequoia National Parks, proposed Kootenai Pass in the far north of the park. Prof. Lyman Sperry, an early explorer of the park and the namesake of Sperry Glacier, proposed Gunsight Pass. George Goodwin, a civil engineer who became acting superintendent of Glacier National Park in 1917, surveyed several routes and convinced National Park Service director Stephen Mather that Logan Pass was the place. He recommended a road from Lake McDonald up over the Continental Divide to St. Mary Lake, a steep climb of about 2,600 feet.

In 1924, Mather came to Glacier to consider two alternate routes. Goodwin suggested a direct climb toward Logan Pass by way of a series of switchbacks. Another set of switchbacks would carry the road down the East Side of Logan Pass to the head of St. Mary Lake. This route required an eight percent maximum grade and sharp, 50-foot-radius curves. Advantages of this proposal were relative ease of construction and economy. Goodwin also believed the extensive switchbacks would be viewed as impressive evidence of man's mastery over nature.

Thomas Vint, the park service landscape engineer, complained that the switchbacks would scar the face of the Lewis Range at its most picturesque, making it look like a strip mine. His alternative was a longer and straighter road. Instead of climbing straight up to Logan Pass, the road would climb away from the pass, then make a single switchback. From there, it would follow a relatively straight and level route across the nearly vertical cliff face of the Lewis Range, known as the Garden Wall, back toward Logan Pass.

Mather brought in the bureau of public roads to supervise the construction. They, in turn, assigned highway engineer Frank Kittredge to survey the routes. Kittredge, who became National Park Service chief engineer in 1927, recommended the Vint route, and Mather concurred. Aesthetics would play an important part in designing and building the road.

Above is a dramatic, late-winter view of the unopened Going-to-the-Sun Road, cutting across the face of the Garden Wall, the part of the Lewis Range of the Rocky Mountains that runs through the center of Glacier National Park. The name came when George Bird Grinnell and his friends were camping in the region and, one evening around a campfire, were singing the then popular

song, "Over the Garden Wall." Someone said, "There is one wall we cannot get over," and the name stuck. The avalanche chutes in the center converge on the course of Haystack Creek. (Courtesy National Park Service.)

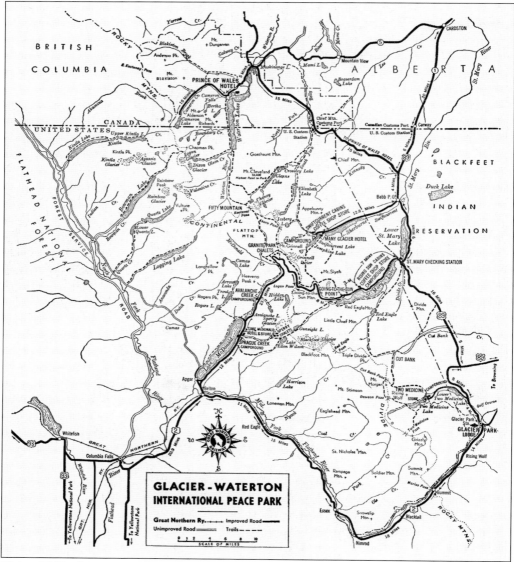

This c. 1940 reference map shows the position of the Going-to-the-Sun Road as the true centerpiece of Glacier National Park, running from Belton (West Glacier since 1949) in the lower left to the St. Mary Checking Station at center right. Note US Highway 2 running parallel to the Great Northern Railway and the southern boundary of the park. Though the map dates from the 1940s, little has changed within the park since the Going-to-the-Sun Road was dedicated in 1933. (Author's collection.)

Roy "Swede" Bengtson, Clyde Fauley, and William J. Yenne, the author's father, are seen here with a bulldozer near Logan Creek at about Mile 20 of the Going-to-the-Sun Road during the extensive program of plowing required to open the Going-to-the-Sun Road each year. This photograph was taken on April 5, 1960, two months before the road was finally open. During the 1960s, William J. Yenne was supervisor of roads in Glacier National Park. Fauley's father-in-law Ray Price had worked on the original construction of the road four decades earlier. Swede had also worked on the Going-to-the-Sun Road construction, starting in 1928, and continued to work seasonally on road maintenance until his retirement in 1979 as Glacier's longest-serving employee. (Yenne family collection.)

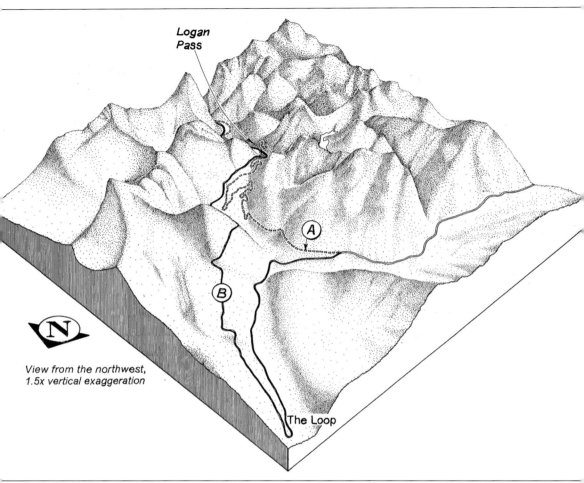

Logan Pass

The Loop

Here are the two final options proposed for routing the Going-to-the-Sun Road. The first (A), proposed by National Park engineer George Goodwin, followed McDonald Creek until it reached the Logan Creek Valley. Here, the road angled right and climbed toward Logan Pass, ascending to the summit in a series of switchbacks. National Park Service landscape architect Thomas Vint protested that Goodwin's switchbacks would horribly scar the scenic Logan Creek Valley. He proposed a longer route (B) ascending gradually from McDonald Creek with one switchback (the "Loop"). National Park Service director Stephen Mather favored Vint's proposal. US Bureau of Public Roads engineer Frank Kittredge surveyed the route. With only slight modifications, Going-to-the-Sun Road was constructed as proposed by Vint and plotted by Kittredge. (Courtesy US Department of the Interior.)

Thomas Chalmers Vint (1894–1967) was the man most responsible for the design and appearance of the infrastructure within America's parks though the critical first four decades of their development. As with other projects in other parks, he insisted that the Going-to-the-Sun Road across Logan Pass should harmonize as much as possible with the surrounding natural environment. In 1923, having worked with landscape architect Daniel Ray Hull on designs for Yosemite National Park, he became assistant landscape engineer for the National Park Service. He later became chief landscape architect for the National Park Service and went on to be the central figure in developing the rustic look of buildings, bridges, and byways in the national parks through the 1940s. In the 1950s, he helped formulate Mission 66, the upgrading of park facilities with a Midcentury Modern feel. (Courtesy National Park Service.)

Stephen Tyng Mather (1867–1930) was a millionaire businessman turned ardent conservationist who was appointed in 1917 as the first director of the National Park Service. In 1915, he had visited Glacier as part of an epic 10,000-mile tour of the western national parks. When he complained to Secretary of the Interior Franklin Lane about conditions in the national parks, Lane wrote back, "If you don't like the way the national parks are run, why don't you come on down to Washington and run them yourself." He agreed to do so for a year and stayed for a dozen. With his assistant and successor, Horace Albright, he created numerous new parks and built the National Park Service into an efficient professional organization. (Courtesy National Park Service.)

A surveyor, possibly Frank Kittredge himself, ponders the future route of the Going-to-the-Sun Road from high on a cliff overlooking the McDonald Valley from a place near the eventual 24-mile mark on the route of the road. The engineering and construction challenges are obvious. (Author's collection.)

Two

BUILDING THE ROAD

In 1925, the firm D.A. Williams & A.R. Douglas of Tacoma, Washington, was selected, with a bid of $869,145, to construct the steep West Side section of the Transmountain Road, or Logan Pass Road, which would cross the Continental Divide at Logan Pass. By then, 29 of the eventual 51 miles had been built, including 10 miles along the north shore of St. Mary Lake and the dozen miles to the head of Lake McDonald.

Their most difficult section was the roughly eight miles across the face of the Garden Wall from the switchback known as the Loop, to Logan Pass. The work consisted of notching the roadway into the cliff and constructing stone retaining walls. Because of the heavy snowfall, the work was seasonal, limited mainly to the summer. After a slow, late start in 1925, about half the work was completed in 1926, with about two thirds done by the end of 1927.

No major construction occurred on the Garden Wall in 1929 and 1930 because of the West Side fire in 1929 and the Great Depression, but some progress was made on the East Side. In 1931 and 1932, the Colonial Building Company of Spokane, Washington, and A.R. Guthrie of Portland Oregon, built the section east of Logan Pass, including the 405-foot East Side Tunnel.

Despite the difficulty of work in such steep and unforgivable terrain, and hazards that ranged from dynamite to marauding grizzly bears, only three men were killed during the construction, one from a fall and two from falling rock. It is remarkable that there were so few deaths.

The 51-mile route across the mountains was opened for traffic and formally dedicated on July 15, 1933. At the dedication, the road was permanently named, with this name coming from nearby Going-to-the-Sun Mountain, which had been named by the explorer Willard Schultz in around 1888. It has been said that "Going-to-the-Sun" comes from a Blackfeet phrase about a spirit "who went back to the sun after his work was done."

Park naturalist George Ruhle is officially credited with first using this name for the road, though former congressman Louis Cramton, a special assistant to Secretary of the Interior Ray Lyman Wilbur, is also said to have suggested "Going-to-the-Sun" as a name.

Park superintendent J.R. Eakin said that the name "gives the impression that in driving this road, autoists will ascend to extreme heights and view sublime panoramas."

This c. 1926 photograph shows construction crews in the vicinity of the Loop, with snowcapped Flattop Mountain in the background. The work involved notching the inside part of the road into the cliff face, then building a retaining wall on the outside. It was slow and painstaking work that required great precision. As former road foreman Bill Dakin writes, "They hauled up compressors to run drills. Miles of switchback trails were built to enable crews and mule teams to haul cement and sand and pipe and drill steel and food and wood and kegs of black powder, cases of dynamite. Trails so steep, loads so heavy the horses had to be rested alternate days." (Author's collection.)

A trail across the face of the Garden Wall naturally preceded the final construction of the Going-to-the-Sun Road. The steepness of the terrain and the challenges of road building here are certainly illustrated by this photograph. Today, the Highline Trail parallels the road in this same area, running several hundred feet above it across the Garden Wall. The Highline Trail begins at Logan Pass, follows the route of the Going-to-the-Sun Road for eight miles, then continues for another dozen miles to the Fifty Mountain Campground. (Author's collection.)

The work is being examined on the West Side below timberline, about a mile or so uphill from Logan Creek, around 1926. Note the Williams & Douglas power shovel in the background. (Bill Dakin collection.)

The Blackfeet leader Mad Wolf ("Siyeh" in Blackfeet), who inducted Walter McClintock into the tribe, is seen here with his wife, Gives-to-the-Sun, in 1905. Wrote McClintock of Mad Wolf, "He had a noble countenance, and a large and shapely head. . . . From his piercing glance and the firm expression of his mouth, I knew he was accustomed to command. . . . From his neck hung a medicine whistle made from the wing-bone of an eagle. In his back hair, a single eagle feather stood erect." Several features within Glacier National Park, including a mountain, glacier and stream, are named Siyeh. (Walter McClintock photograph; courtesy US Department of the Interior.)

Three

THE BLACKFEET

Long before the mountains of the Crown of the Continent were tread by the boots of explorers, such as Lyman Sperry, Willard Schultz and George Bird Grinnell, they formed the backdrop for the lives and traditional homeland of the Blackfeet people. They have lived in the plains and valleys immediately east of the park for centuries, and their reservation is located here today. They have long considered these mountains, which form the western backdrop to their homeland, to be the "Backbone of the World." When compared to the vast open plains to the east, it is easy to understand why.

The sun plays an important role in the cosmology of the Blackfeet. Walter McClintock, who first went to Montana with a US Forest Service expedition in 1896, stayed on to spend several years living with the Blackfeet, writing about their culture at a time when it was far more intact that it would be by the 1920s.

"The Sun, as the great center of power and the upholder of all things, was the Blackfeet's supreme object of worship," writes McClintock in his book, *The Old North Trail*. He continues:

He saw that every bud and leaf and blossom turned its face towards the Sun as the source of its life and growth; that the berries he ate reddened and ripened under its warmth; that men and animals thrived under its sustaining light, but all perished when it was withdrawn. He saw that in the darkness and cold of winter, nature retired into silence and sleep; that when the sunlight and warmth of spring returned, all nature awakened and put on its robe of green; the bears left their hibernating dens and the beavers their winter lodges. The Sun made the grass to grow and the trees to be covered with foliage for the subsistence of birds and animals, upon which he himself in turn depended for food. The devout Blackfoot therefore called upon men, women and children and everything that had breath to worship the all-glorious, all-powerful, Sun-God who fills the heavens with brightness and the earth with life and beauty. To them, he is the supreme source of light, of life, and of power.

A group of Blackfeet cross the prairie on their way to a ceremony in the fall of 1904, with the Rocky Mountains of the future Glacier National Park visible in the distance. (Walter McClintock photograph; courtesy US Department of the Interior.)

Anatapsa (Mad Wolf's granddaughter) and her friend Dives-Under-Water are seen here near the future eastern terminus of the Going-to-the-Sun Road in 1909. Wrote McClintock, "Anatapsa, gaily dressed, sat in front, her long black hair flying in the wind. Her blanket of brilliant scarlet fell loosely from her shoulders, confined at the waist by a belt heavily beaded. . . . Dives-under-water, clothed in a robe of soft-tanned fawn skin with beaded stripes, was seated behind. She was deaf and dumb but full of life and skilled in the sign language. Her busy hands moved gracefully while talking with Anatapsa. From their mischievous looks and frequent peals of laughter, I knew their jokes were at the expense of those around them." (Walter McClintock photograph; courtesy US Department of the Interior.)

Seen here are two 1907 views of a Blackfeet hunting camp on the eastern edge of what later became Glacier National Park. The bottom photograph was taken the next morning after an early fall snowfall. (Walter McClintock photographs; courtesy US Department of the Interior.)

This view, looking north from atop the railroad underpass, shows the first half-mile of the Going-to-the-Sun Road through Belton (now West Glacier) as it has appeared since 1939. Built as matching structures, the post office and the three West Glacier Mercantile buildings are on the left, and the gas station owned by the Mercantile Company is on the right. All of these building still remain. The railings of the 1939 bridge into the park can be seen just beyond. In the background is Apgar Mountain with the fire lookout at the top. The mountain was severely ravaged by forest fires in 1929 and 2003. (Courtesy Bill Lundgren, West Glacier Mercantile Company.)

This view of the West Glacier Mercantile Company (then Belton Mercantile Company) shows the buildings from the opposite direction. From left to right, they are the post office, gift shop, grocery store, and café. The only difference between this view and one today is the addition of tall deciduous trees, which have grown up in the median between the Going-to-the-Sun Road and the street in front of the buildings. (Courtesy, Bill Lundgren, West Glacier Mercantile Company.)

Four

THE WEST ENTRANCE

The Going-to-the-Sun Road is usually described from west to east because the earliest precursor segment was the 19th-century wagon road from the Great Northern Railway depot at Belton to the foot of Lake McDonald in the late 19th century. Belton, officially renamed West Glacier on October 1, 1949, is the western gateway to the Going-to-the-Sun Road and to Glacier National Park. The tracks of the Great Northern Railway reached Belton in 1891, and the company built its Belton Chalets here in 1910. Across the tracks, the Belton (later West Glacier) Mercantile Company built a number of commercial buildings that have been in use since 1939.

The Going-to-the-Sun Road effectively begins at its junction with US Highway 2, where it passes under the railroad tracks (now Burlington Northern Santa Fe) and near the West Glacier Mercantile buildings. The Glacier National Park boundary comes a quarter of a mile from Highway 2 at the bridge crossing the Middle Fork of the Flathead River. The present entrance station, completed in 1941, is less than a mile farther on. Prior to 1939, the road crossed into the park about a mile farther east (upriver) and the entrance station was inside Park Headquarters, which has been bypassed by the Going-to-the-Sun Road since 1939.

About a mile inside the park, travelers reach the foot of Lake McDonald and Apgar Village, which grew up around a number of early homesteads established in the 1890s. Before the creation of the park in 1910, men such as Frank Kelly and Charlie Howe, as well as Milo, Harvey, and Dimon Apgar, operated tourist cabins in the area. Noted Western artist Charles M. "Charley" Russell maintained a summer home in Apgar, which he called Bull Head Lodge. Frank Geduhn, meanwhile, had a large and fondly remembered tourist camp at the head of the lake.

Most of the original private owners have long since sold their property to the National Park Service, but some homes and businesses continue to exist in Apgar today. Apgar is a bustling place in the summer months but has few year-round residents.

The West Glacier Mercantile Food Market has little changed since 1939. (Photograph by the author.)

This photograph shows the historic West Glacier Post Office (located at the far left in the photographs on page 25) at the time the author mailed his last postcard here in 1999. It was superseded by a new building a few dozen feet to the south, but this building still exists. The post office once was an essential link to the outside world. In those years, long distance telephone calls were complicated and expensive and were routed through an operator halfway across the state. Even today, cell phone reception is problematic here. (Photograph by the author.)

Located to the south, across the railroad tracks from the mercantile complex, the Belton Chalets were built by the Great Northern Railway and opened in 1911. An annex with two dozen additional guest rooms opened on the hill above the main building in 1913. They were sold by the Great Northern in 1946. (Courtesy Bill Lundgren, West Glacier Mercantile Company.)

After a half-century succession of private owners, the Belton Chalets were acquired in 1997 by Andy Baxter and Cas Still and restored to their former glory. In the 1960s, the hotel was boarded up, and the restaurant operated as Peter Pence's Pizza Parlor. (Photograph by the author.)

Built in 1920, the concrete arch bridge at Belton was the only major highway access to the West Side of Glacier National Park for nearly two decades. Designed by George Goodwin, who planned the Going-to-the-Sun Road, it was built by Charles McClung in 1920, replacing a nearby log bridge dating to about 1897. Though superseded by a large steel frame bridge in 1939, it continued to be used well into the 1960s. (Author's collection.)

This dramatic photograph shows the last minutes before the upper portion of the 1920 concrete bridge was obliterated by heavy logs carried in the surging flood waters of the Middle Fork of the Flathead River on June 8, 1964. Long considered to have been Montana's worst natural disaster, the Great Flood of June 1964 began with a snowstorm in Glacier, and snowpack-melting rainfall in double-digit depth all across the western part of Montana. It ended with $62 million in damage and the death of more than 30 people, most of them on the Blackfeet Reservation along Glacier's eastern boundary. (Photograph by the author.)

The Great Flood of June 1964 wiped out everything but the arch of the 1920 concrete arch bridge. However, the flood had essentially destroyed the newer steel bridge, so the National Park Service installed a wooden superstructure, and the Going-to-the-Sun Road was open by June 30 using the old bridge. Since the other bridge was replaced, the road leading into the park from the old bridge was closed, and this bridge has been used only as a pedestrian crossing. (Photograph by the author.)

The author (right) and a friend are seen here on the Going-to-the-Sun Road as it crosses the 1939 steel bridge over the Middle Fork of the Flathead River at West Glacier, about a mile downstream from the 1920 bridge (top picture). This January 1953 photograph can be compared to the one at the top of page 32. The entrance sign is located at the bend in the road in the distance. (Doris Yenne photograph.)

Photographs of the 1939 steel bridge show the effects of the Great Flood of June 1964. Above, a downstream view shows the collapsed center section; below, an upstream view shows the structure filled with logs. The logs caused the resistance that broke the bridge. (Photographs by the author.)

These photographs also show the effects of the Great Flood of 1964 on the 1939 steel bridge. Above, the same view (as the bottom of page 30) shows the logs removed; below, the bridge is pictured as it was being disassembled. It was replaced by another bridge in the same location. (Photographs by the author.)

The author stands before the West Entrance sign on the park side of the Middle Fork Bridge on a snowy April day in 2011. This was the year of the latest opening of the Going-to-the-Sun Road to date (July 13), six weeks later than in the flood year of 1964. (Author's collection.)

There has been a succession of dozens of different sign styles at the park entrances (see pages 120 to 121). This one, created by park sign maker Dave Yeats, was installed in 2006. (David Restivo, National Park Service.)

This old log building in Park Headquarters, seen here in December 1953, was the official West Entrance Station of Glacier National Park from about 1916 to 1941. It was converted to employee housing thereafter. The author lived here from 1953 to 1958. The original route of the Going-to-the-Sun Road is visible on the right. (Courtesy Yenne family collection.)

The author (center) and friends hang out in the backyard of the house pictured above in February 1956. Because of the deep snowfall (much deeper at higher elevations), it is typical for deer, and occasionally elk, to winter in among the homes and National Park Service offices at Park Headquarters. (Doris Yenne photograph.)

The author and his mother pause for a photograph in front of the "old Apgar home" in February 1954. Milo, Harvey, and Dimon "Dimie" Apgar were among the early homesteaders in the area, which has borne their name for more than a century. Harvey donated the land for the Apgar School, and the town is said to have been named for him. Many of the original pioneer homes around Apgar were destroyed in the enormous 1929 forest fire, while others were acquired by the National Park Service through the 1960s and demolished. This was the era when historic preservation was taken less seriously as a mandate of the agency than it would be later. (William J. Yenne photograph.)

Shown is the main street of Apgar Village looking north, with the foot of Lake McDonald visible at the end. The old growth cedars in this area survived the forest fires of 1929 and 2003, which came precariously close. (Photograph by the author.)

This 1979 photograph was taken a city block farther from the lake than the one at opposite, bottom. In this era, the National Park Service had replaced earlier rustic and personalized signage with uniform signs set in the Craw Clarendon typeface. (Photograph by the author.)

This photograph (the same view as above) was taken in 2006 after a softening liberalization of government signage requirements. (Photograph by the author.)

Eddie's Café is one of Glacier's longest-lived and best-loved commercial institutions. It is named for Eddie Brewster, who purchased a small grocery store in Apgar Village in 1946. He later expanded, adding the café, which he operated until 1972. For the next several decades, it was operated by Donna and Jerry Larson. Eddie's father, Horace Brewster, came to Apgar in 1910 when Eddie was a little boy. Horace Brewster worked for Charley Russell for a time and later served as Glacier's first park ranger. (Photograph by the author.)

These travelers are waiting for a Going-to-the-Sun Road shuttle at the Apgar transit center. In 2007, this long-overdue addition to park transportation was carved out of a lodgepole pine forest that had grown up after the 1929 fire. (David Restivo, National Park Service.)

This view from the boat dock at the foot of Lake McDonald shows the lake framed against the mountains. The opening in the mountains just above the left boat is the upper McDonald Valley. (Photograph by the author.)

A black bear begs at a car. This was a common sight and favorite photograph opportunity along the Going-to-the-Sun Road in the McDonald Valley and, indeed, in most western national parks through the 1950s. Travelers have long been strongly discouraged from the practice. It is not only dangerous, it encourages bears to favor human food, making them more aggressive around people and less able to forage for themselves in the wild. (Rev. M.J. McPike.)

The mountains that rise above the upper McDonald Valley are reflected in Lake McDonald. To the right are Mount Cannon (8,952 feet), Mount Brown (8,565 feet), and the Little Matterhorn (7,886 feet). At the distant head of the McDonald Valley, partly shrouded by clouds, is the Garden Wall, which is traversed by the Going-to-the-Sun Road. (Photograph by the author.)

Except at midday during the busy summer months, the upper McDonald Valley can provide excellent wildlife viewing, including such megafauna as moose and black bears. At Mile 14 on the Going-to-the-Sun Road, deep in the forest among the old growth cedars of the upper McDonald Valley, beaver long ago dammed streams coming off Mount Brown, creating a swamp, which has been enjoyed for countless generations of moose. Through the years, the National Park Service has alternated between celebrating this "Moose Habitat" with extensive signage along the Going-to-the-Sun Road and ignoring it by removing the signs completely. (Photograph by the author.)

Stanton Mountain (7,750 feet) rises along the western head of Lake McDonald, directly across the McDonald Valley from Mount Brown. According to the official Glacier National Park administrative history, it is named for Lottie Stanton, "a pioneer woman who followed the construction camps during the railroad building days." Mount Brown is named for William Brown of Chicago, an executive with the Chicago & Alton Railroad who climbed it while camping and fishing around Lake McDonald in 1894. Mount Cannon is named for a young couple who climbed the mountain while on their honeymoon. In 1894, Lyman Sperry had named it Goat Mountain because its slopes abound with mountain goats. The Little Matterhorn is so-named because of its similarity to the famous Matterhorn in Switzerland, which is nearly twice as tall. (Photograph by the author.)

Glacier National Park's signature buses have been a familiar sight along the Going-to-the-Sun Road since 1936. They have been known variously as Red Buses (their color), White Buses (their manufacturer, the White Motor Company), or Jammer Buses (drivers used to have to double-clutch and "jam" the gears of the original manual transmissions when climbing the steep Going-to-the-Sun). The Jammer Buses were originally acquired by the Great Northern Railway to take patrons to their chain of hotels and chalets and on tours across Logan Pass on the Going-to-the-Sun Road. Once scheduled for retirement, 32 of the buses were retrofitted with automatic transmissions in 1989, and with modern Ford van chassis and propane-fueled engines from 2000 to 2002. Here, a driver rolls back the convertible canvas top in preparation for a run on the Going-to-the-Sun Road from the Lake McDonald Lodge. (Photograph by the author.)

The facade of the Lake McDonald Lodge is little changed since the building was constructed (1913–1914) by John Lewis. It is the only one of the three grand lodges of Glacier National Park that is located near the Going-to-the-Sun Road. The turnoff for the lodge is located at Mile 10, almost at the head of Lake McDonald. Designed for Lewis by the Spokane firm of Kirtland, Cutter, and Malmgren, the property was acquired in 1930 by the Great Northern Railway, which built and operated Glacier's other lodges. Now owned by the National Park Service, it is operated by Glacier Park, Inc. (Courtesy US Department of the Interior.)

Pictured is the interior of the Lake McDonald Lodge as John Lewis decorated it, with artifacts from his years of trading with trappers in the region. Though many of these artifacts were pilfered through the years, a sizable number still adorn the lobby today. (Author's collection.)

This 1908 photograph of the upper McDonald Valley was taken long before surveyors came to Going-to-the-Sun Road. However, so little has changed through the past century, it could have been taken from the road last summer. Only a few steps from a busy thoroughfare, the wilderness is as pristine today as it was when humans first arrived. (Walter McClintock photograph; courtesy US Department of the Interior.)

The Going-to-the-Sun Road is barely visible on the right, cutting through the trees above the banks of upper McDonald Creek. The flood plain in the foreground is a reminder of the 1964 flooding, although McDonald Creek is much higher each spring than it appears in this photograph. (Courtesy US Department of the Interior.)

A wary wolf keeps an eye on Going-to-the-Sun Road snow-clearing crews in the early spring. In the summer, this may be a busy thoroughfare, but for most of the year, there are no people whatsoever here, and the upper McDonald Valley belongs to the wild. Wolves were hunted (with a bounty) inside the park until 1934, resulting in their absence for half a century. A growing number of packs have reestablished themselves here since the 1980s. (Courtesy National Park Service.)

Each year by April, the plowing of the Going-to-the-Sun Road typically reaches about 15 miles into the upper McDonald Valley, note the Garden Wall in the background. Compare the snow depth here to the depth of snow at higher elevations as seen in the photographs on the following pages. (Courtesy National Park Service.)

With McDonald Creek on the left, a rotary snowplow makes its way along the Going-to-the-Sun Road near Red Rock Point at about Mile 17.4, between Avalanche Creek and Logan Creek. The annual opening of the road often reaches this point in April. (Courtesy National Park Service.)

This photograph captures a westbound traveler on the Going-to-the-Sun Road in the vicinity of Logan Creek, with the Garden Wall rising above, in the 1970s. The path of the road can be seen cutting across the Garden Wall about halfway up. The white water of a falls on Haystack Creek is visible at right center. By August, the largely snow-free Garden Wall is a much different place than it is for most of the year. (Courtesy US Department of the Interior.)

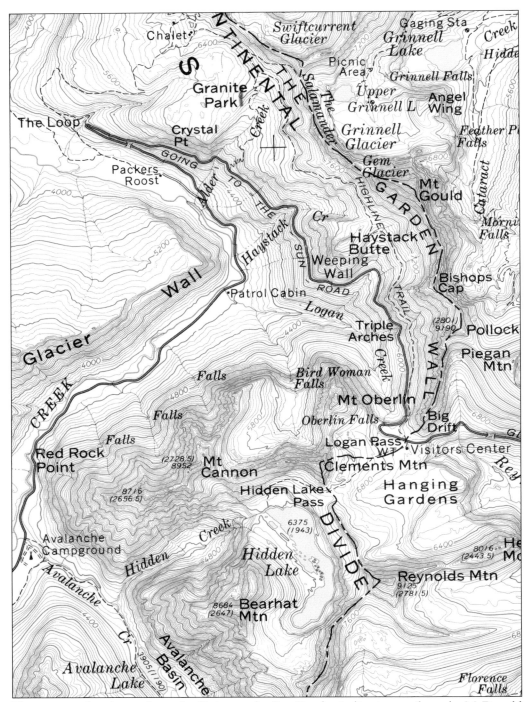

This topographical map shows the Going-to-the-Sun Road, winding its way from the McDonald Valley to Logan Pass and beyond. The Loop is at the top left, with the interrupted road denoting the West Side Tunnel just below. The East Side Tunnel is seen on the right as the road descends past the Big Drift from Logan Pass. (Courtesy US Geological Survey.)

50

Six

THE WEST SIDE
TO LOGAN PASS

The Going-to-the-Sun Road climbs only about 500 feet in elevation in the nine miles between Lake McDonald and Logan Creek. However, it then begins a steady six-percent climb out of the valley, gaining nearly 1,000 feet in the roughly four miles from Logan Creek (Mile 21.2) to the Loop (Mile 24.7). The latter is the major switchback, which reverses the direction of the Going-to-the-Sun Road from northwest to southeast. Climbing above the Loop, the road is cut into the face of the Garden Wall, climbing more than 2,200 feet in the eight miles to Logan Pass.

Logan Creek was the site of the Williams & Douglas Construction Camp No. 1, the first of several from which the company operated simultaneously. Three miles from here is the turnoff for the Packer's Roost, which is the trailhead for the Fifty Mountain Trail. It is so-named because packers bringing pack strings into the backcountry before the Going-to-the-Sun Road was built would spend the night here.

Above Logan Creek, at Mile 24, travelers pass through the 192-foot West Side Tunnel, one of two tunnels on the Going-to-the-Sun Road. It is notable for the two large arched windows, or "viewing galleries," that afford glimpses of Heavens Peak (8,987 feet) across the valley. The tunnel was constructed in 1926 by H.W. Bennett and Phil Segolia, subcontractors to Williams & Douglas.

Williams & Douglas built 7,242 linear feet of retaining wall. W.G. Peters, writing in *Western Construction News* in 1929, notes that "to ensure stability, most of the retaining walls were built with a triangular cross section with the base equaling one-half the height of the wall. Very few of Williams & Douglas' retaining walls, particularly those on straight sections of road, exceeded 11 feet in height because of the base-to-height ratio."

There were many nationalities involved in the construction. "Italians were involved with many of the masonry guardrails. Another employee recalled A.R. Douglas' tendency to hire his fellow Irish [hard rock miners] from Butte," Kathryn Steen wrote in a 1990 official Historic American Engineering Record history of the road. "The Russians [based at Camp Six, had] their own cook tent and their own cook. They were subcontractors on the Garden Wall section."

The contractors tended to hire small numbers of skilled workers rather than large numbers of inexpensive unskilled laborers. Ira Stinson, the engineer at Glacier National Park from 1932 to 1951, recalled that, "This was a job for experts from the ground up."

Here is a Williams & Douglas power shovel at work just below the Loop in 1925. This photograph puzzled many who wondered how the shovel reached this location when the West Side Tunnel below had not yet been finished. In 1983, at the 50th-anniversary reunion of the men who built the Going-to-the-Sun Road, Bill Dakin had occasion to meet stonemason George Jimm, who explained that they had cut a light-impact tote road up from the Packer's Roost. "After he told us that, sure enough, we could find evidence of the road," Dakin recalls. "Getting that shovel up there was a huge task, but it meant everything for getting construction done both ways from the Loop and meant a whole season of progress while the tunnel was being built." (Bill Dakin collection.)

This snow-removal equipment at work on the Going-to-the-Sun Road is in roughly the same area that the photograph below was taken. The drifts are still shoulder deep along this section in April. (Courtesy National Park Service.)

This photograph, taken along the Going-to-the-Sun Road between the Packer's Roost Road and the West Side Tunnel in July, shows the path cut by an especially large avalanche that came off the Garden Wall the previous winter, bringing tons of deadfall with it. Crews anticipate such challenges as a routine park of opening the road. In late 2006, however, heavy rainfall and major flooding caused washouts and bridge damage along the Going-to-the-Sun Road, which imposed additional complications and expenses to the process. (Photograph by the author.)

53

This c. 1938 photograph shows a then new Red Bus parked just uphill from the West Side Tunnel, with two men pausing to have a look. This is one of the myriad waterfalls that pours from the never-melted snowfields high on the Garden Wall all summer long. Mount Oberlin (8,180 feet) forms a majestic backdrop. (Author's collection.)

The West Side Tunnel's two large archways, cut out on the south side (right), cast light on snow-clearing equipment inside. (Courtesy National Park Service.)

This view looks uphill into the West Side Tunnel. Carved through solid limestone, the tunnel, as originally constructed, was 192 feet long, 20 feet wide, and 18 feet high. In the winter of 1966 to 1967, after the close of the travel season, crews worked to widen the tunnel. (Courtesy US Department of the Interior.)

One of the two "windows" cut into the west side of the West Side Tunnel can be seen in this photograph of a signature Red Bus parked inside (as drivers are officially admonished not to do). A wonderful view of Heavens Peak is framed by this opening. (David Restivo, National Park Service.)

This view, at about Mile 24.6, looking westward toward the West Side Tunnel and McDonald Creek, shows a rotary snowplow at work on the Going-to-the-Sun Road just below the Loop. At the landmark switchback, the road switches direction and heads toward 6,646-foot Logan Pass, which is seen as the cleft between the mountains directly above the snowplow. (Courtesy National Park Service.)

The loop of "the Loop" is seen in this photograph, which also shows the lodgepole pine that were burned in the 2003 Trapper Fire. Much of the same area that burned in 2003 had previously burned in the 1936 Heavens Peak Fire. The sign marks the trailhead for a four-mile trail leading to the Granite Park Chalet. (Photograph by the author.)

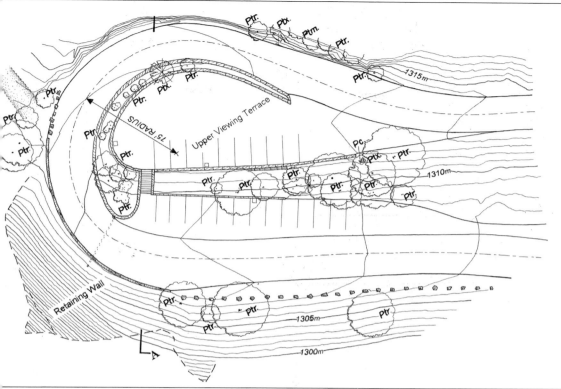

This is the site plan of the Loop and adjacent parking areas as laid out and constructed in 1933. The upper parking area is framed by the switchback made by the hairpin turn of the Going-to-the-Sun Road rounding the Loop, while the lower (downhill) parking area is next to the road on the left. Bill Dakin writes of talented stonemason George Jimm, "who didn't like bosses and didn't work well with others, so foreman Russell Smith put him to work at the Loop all alone and he laid every rock in the walls and stairway by himself." (Historic American Engineering Record, drawn by Christopher A. Boldt.)

This dramatic view of Heavens Peak (8,987 feet) was taken looking southward from the Loop. The mountain was named by Lt. George Ahern on an early map that he drew of the area that became Glacier National Park. He was a member of a US Army expedition that passed though (1888–1890). A glacier, mountain, and mountain pass in Glacier are all named for Ahern. (Photograph by the author.)

This photograph, taken from near the Loop looking east toward Logan Pass, shows the route of the Going-to-the-Sun Road across the face of the Garden Wall on the left and travels behind Mount Oberlin (8,180 feet). The top of Clements Mountain (8,760 feet) can be seen on the right. Also visible to the right of Mount Oberlin is 492-foot Bird Woman Falls. It is named for Sacajawea (also spelled "Sacagawea"), the Shoshone teenager who proved to be an indispensable member of the Lewis and Clark Expedition. Her name means "Bird Woman" in Hidatsa, the language of the tribe who kidnapped her from her home as a child. Neither she, nor any member of the expedition ever saw the falls. (Photograph by the author.)

Rounding Crystal Point at Mile 25.3 heading westbound, downhill toward the Loop, the traveler has an excellent straight-on view of Heavens Peak. (Photograph by the author.)

This recent view shows the same area as the image on the facing page. While the retaining walls and guardrails on the Going-to-the-Sun Road were originally constructed of mortared stone, current construction practices call for them to be built of reinforced concrete and faced with stone veneer. When he was overseeing the planning for the Going-to-the-Sun Road, as well as for similar roads in Yosemite National Park in the 1920s, Thomas Vint was emphatic about using stone quarried from the same area. The 21st-century project is part of the Western Federal Lands Highway Program. The work is managed by the Federal Highway Administration, a successor to the Bureau of Public Roads that oversaw the construction of the Going-to-the-Sun Road eight decades earlier. (Courtesy US Department of Transportation.)

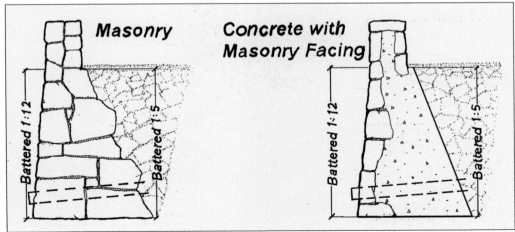

These cross sections illustrate the differences between the vintage 1920s stone-and-mortar retaining wall and guardrail structure (left) and the reinforced concrete structures used today (above). In both cases, native stone from the immediate area is used on the face to harmonize the man-made features with their surrounding environment. (Courtesy Historic American Engineering Record, drawn by Lucas Dupuis.)

Snow is removed on the Going-to-the-Sun Road in the vicinity of Haystack Creek every spring. The photograph on pages 10–11 shows a distant view of snow accumulation in the area where the road crosses Haystack Creek. (Courtesy National Park Service.)

This detail view is of the single arch of the Haystack Creek Culvert, located at Mile 26. It was constructed by Williams & Douglas in 1926 using native limestone. The Historic American Engineering Record reports that it is "a concrete slab culvert with a masonry facade." The arch is 12 feet high at its apex and 16 feet wide. A timber and steel rail was installed atop the stone guardrail in 1968. The single archway is an architectural foretaste to the famous Triple Arches about a mile farther east. (Courtesy US Department of the Interior.)

George Alexander Grant, a great National Park Service photographer, took this image of the Haystack Creek bend as he drove the unpaved Going-to-the-Sun Road to attend the formal dedication in 1933. (Courtesy National Park Service.)

A bulldozer rounds the curve above Haystack Creek as the Going-to-the-Sun Road begins to go around Haystack Butte. The way that the original 1926 guardrails blend into the surrounding stone is clearly evident in this image. (Courtesy National Park Service.)

This view shows the deep snowdrift on the ground at the location of the former Garden Wall Road Camp, at Mile 27 on the Going-to-the-Sun Road. Originally known as Camp Nine during the construction of the road, it stills serves as a park service road camp. However, it has been greatly downsized since the 1960s, and most of the buildings have been removed. (Courtesy National Park Service.)

This photograph faces westward, back down the Going-to-the-Sun Road toward Haystack Butte and the Garden Wall Road Camp. The condition of the guardrail before the turn-of-the-century reconstruction can be seen in the foreground. (Courtesy US Department of the Interior.)

The Garden Wall Road Camp is pictured here during its heyday in the fall of 1959. There was also housing located across the road. (Photograph by the author.)

Crews install stone veneer panels near Haystack Creek during the Western Federal Lands Highway Program retaining wall and guardrail project on the Going-to-the-Sun Road. (Courtesy US Department of Transportation.)

Crews pour concrete as a base for a new guardrail during the Western Federal Lands Highway Program reconstruction of the Going-to-the-Sun Road in 2009. This is the western side of Haystack Butte. (Courtesy US Department of Transportation.)

This old mortared stone guardrail, much of which had deteriorated by the 1990s, is located near Haystack Creek. (Courtesy US Department of the Interior.)

Sections of crumbling guardrail were often revealed during the spring road opening. During the long winters, avalanches, as well as the contractions and expansions of the stone that come with freezing, can take their toll on mortared stone and stone-veneered concrete. (Courtesy National Park Service.)

Asphalt paving work is seen here at Mile 29.5 along the Going-to-the-Sun Road in the vicinity of the Weeping Wall as part of the Western Federal Lands Highway Program. (Courtesy US Department of Transportation.)

Gerald "Gary" Yates (1932–2007) was a noted outdoorsman, mountain climber, and a veteran National Park Service road crewman on the Going-to-the-Sun Road. The photograph on the left was taken at Crystal Point with Heavens Peak in the background. The one on the right was taken at Haystack Creek, with the culvert visible in the background. Born the same year that the Going-to-the-Sun Road was being completed, he worked here seasonally for many summers as well as putting in time at Pecos National Monument in New Mexico. He retired in 1995. (Both, courtesy Bill Dakin.)

This is a view of the Going-to-the-Sun Road about four miles above Haystack Creek, rounding the bend toward the Triple Arches area. (Courtesy US Department of the Interior.)

Pictured is rock scaling work being done on the Going-to-the-Sun Road under the Western Federal Lands Highway Program of the Western Federal Lands Highway Division. (Courtesy US Department of Transportation.)

This is an example of the seasonal timber and steel guardrail as installed during and after 1968. It was removed at the end of the season (to prevent it from being destroyed by avalanches during the winter) and was reinstalled each spring. (Courtesy US Department of the Interior.)

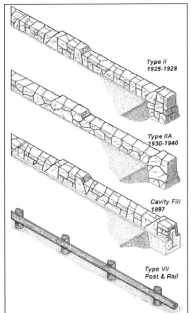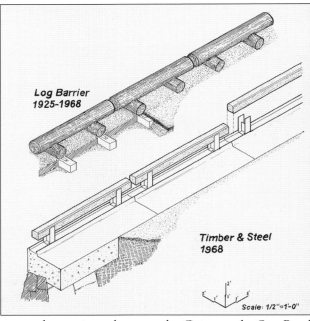

These illustrations show guardrail types used at various places on the Going-to-the-Sun Road through the years. Those on the left were installed permanently. Those on the right were seasonal and removable guardrails. The Type II crenellated stone masonry guard is characterized by a random rubble mosaic pattern with transverse and longitudinal jointing in the top course and large stones at the crenellations. The Type IIA is characterized by a roughly squared rubble pattern with only transverse jointing in the top course. The Type VII post-and-rail guard rail was a standard National Park Service design used in Glacier primarily at waysides. (Both, courtesy Historic American Engineering Record, drawn by Lucas Dupuis.)

As the plowing progresses, the Going-to-the-Sun Road can be used by regular vehicle (though not yet public) traffic traveling one way. (Courtesy National Park Service.)

Even in the late summer, it is not uncommon for slabs of snow to turn the Going-to-the-Sun Road back into a one-way street. (Photograph by the author.)

Travelers who have climbed the Going-to-the-Sun Road to the Garden Wall are given an opportunity to pause and look back to where they had come in the previous six miles of driving. Here, the Going-to-the-Sun Road is visible as it parallels McDonald Creek in the upper McDonald Valley, roughly 2,500 feet below. Compare this photograph to the one on page 49, looking the other way. (Photograph by the author.)

The famous Weeping Wall is located at Mile 27.6 on the Going-to-the-Sun Road. This popular feature is a favorite for youngsters in westbound cars because they can reach out the window and get their hands wet in the cool run-off from snow fields high above, as their parents fumble unexpectedly for windshield wiper levers. (Both, courtesy National Park Service.)

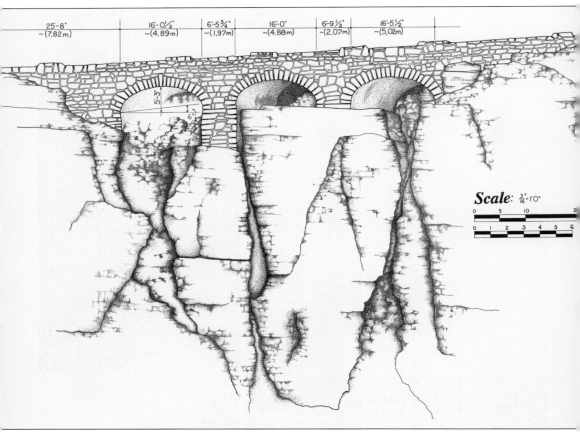

| 25'-8" ~(7,82m) | 16'-0½" ~(4,89m) | 6'-5¾" ~(1,97m) | 16'-0" ~(4,88m) | 6'-9½" ~(2,07m) | 16'-5½" ~(5,02m) |

5'-3"

6'

Scale: 3/16"=1'0"

0   5   10   2

0   1   2   3   4   5   6

This detailed drawing illustrates the dimensions of the various elements of the 1927 engineering marvel at Mile 30.4 that is known as the Triple Arches. The arches are a substitute for a retaining wall and are built as half culverts. The arches support only part of the road's width. No water runs under them. As described by Kathryn Steen in the Historic American Engineering Record: "Changes in the construction plans at the Triple Arches site were probably discussed with and approved by the resident landscape architect Ernest A. Davidson, but he apparently did not see the actual working plans until the arches were already under construction. As a result, the contractors built the first arch—the one on the downhill side away from Logan Pass—with the arch's spring line (the imaginary line connecting the base points of the curves) parallel to the six percent grade of the road instead of running horizontally." Davidson corrected the error when constructing the next two arches; he felt the error in the first arch would not be noticeable to most visitors. (Historic American Engineering Record, drawn by William Withers and Albert Debnam.)

As noted by Kathryn Steen in the Historic American Engineering Record, "The contractors were faced with building a solid retaining wall in excess of 20 feet in depth. In order to create a stable wall, the contractor would have had to excavate a massive amount of material at the base. Instead, the contractor . . . or more likely . . . one of their subcontractors, developed on-site the less expensive plan for the Triple Arches to span the rifts of the mountain face. The new plan incorporated the solid rock cliffs and ledges of Pollock Mountain as bases for the arches of the retaining wall, thus eliminating the need for costly and time consuming excavation." (Courtesy US Department of the Interior.)

By the middle of June, the Triple Arches area is mostly clear of snow, and crews can begin installing the removable seasonal guardrails. (Courtesy National Park Service.)

This dramatic photograph shows snow removal at the Triple Arches with the bulldozer as much as six feet above the road bed, and nothing between it and a 1,000-foot fall. (Courtesy National Park Service.)

This is the view looking eastward into the Triple Arches bend in the Going-to-the-Sun Road before the beginning of snow removal activities. (Courtesy National Park Service.)

These views show a bulldozer at work above the Triple Arches with Reynolds Mountain (9,125 feet) forming the backdrop. In the distance, the line of the Going-to-the-Sun Road is visible as it climbs the last mile to Logan Pass. (Both, courtesy National Park Service.)

This is the spectacular view from the Big Bend at Mile 31 on the Going-to-the-Sun Road. Looking westward, Oberlin Mountain (8,180 feet) frames the view on the left, with a more distant Heavens Peak (8,987 feet) in the center and the shoulder of Haystack Butte (7,486 feet) on the right. (Courtesy National Park Service.)

The snow drifts deeper and lasts longer as a large patch at the Big Bend than at any other place on the Going-to-the-Sun Road between the Loop and Logan Pass. (Courtesy National Park Service.)

This photograph of the Big Bend Area was taken from high above as crews plow both the Going-to-the-Sun Road and the expansive parking area located here. The large, open expanse at the Big Bend allows more elbow room to stop to enjoy the view than anywhere else on the steep slopes between the Loop and Logan Pass. (Courtesy National Park Service.)

The Going-to-the-Sun Road is pictured passing through the Big Bend area in late summer. The large snowbank at the left usually remains intact until August, if not all summer, affording visitors an opportunity to pause and make snowballs. (Photograph by the author.)

This photograph provides a dramatic illustration of how deep the snowdrifts are at the Big Bend. It is easy to imagine that parts of this massive snowbank would survive all year long. (Courtesy National Park Service.)

In 1933, National Park Service photographer George Alexander Grant visited Glacier National Park for the Going-to-the-Sun Road dedication. On his way up to Logan Pass, he paused to capture the iconic Big Bend snowbank, as well as this traveler with a unique recreational vehicle. (Courtesy National Park Service.)

For many years, a blue grouse nested near a Going-to-the-Sun vehicle turnout along the Garden Wall. To dissuade humans from disturbing her nest, she proactively attacked them if they lingered too long. (Photograph by the author.)

Grizzlies, the most feared and most mesmerizing large mammals in the Glacier ecosystem, tend to move into the backcountry during the summer, and are rarely seen (never say "never") near the Going-to-the-Sun Road. However, during the spring, when they emerge from hibernation, it is another matter. The 400-pound grizzly goes anywhere he or she wants to. This pair was spotted by a road crew on a snowbank covering the road near the Big Bend. (Courtesy National Park Service.)

These bighorn sheep, on the Going-to-the-Sun Road just east of the Big Bend, act like they own the road. For most of the year, they do. (Courtesy National Park Service.)

A spotter standing at the Oberlin Bend (Mile 32) maintains a watch for the threat of an avalanche while a distant bulldozer pioneers the Rimrock area, the last steep section of the Going-to-the-Sun Road's West Side before it passes through the bend and reaches Logan Pass at Mile 32.6. (Courtesy National Park Service.)

This view shows the delicate snow removal work among the vertical cliffs of the Rimrock. (Courtesy National Park Service.)

This photograph was taken from the Highline Trail looking down at the Going-to-the-Sun Road as it enters the Rimrock. (Courtesy National Park Service.)

A 1950s traffic jam ensues at Logan Pass, as motorists stop and passengers spill out of Red Buses, anxious for a fistful of snow and probably a few snowfall fights. (Author's collection.)

An example of Mission 66 architecture, the Logan Pass Visitor Center was designed by Brinkman & Lenon and built between 1963 and 1966. (Courtesy National Park Service.)

Snowplows reach Logan Pass. This photograph was taken at the same place as the one opposite, with Oberlin Mountain in the background. (Courtesy National Park Service.)

Each winter, snowdrifts cover most of the Logan Pass Visitor Center. (Courtesy National Park Service.)

The final stages of the annual snow removal are pictured at the huge parking lot located adjacent to the 6,646-foot Logan Pass, the apogee of the Going-to-the-Sun Road. Looking east, Going-to-the-Sun Mountain (9,642 feet) can be seen prominently in the center background. (Courtesy National Park Service.)

This photograph of the Logan Pass parking lot was taken around the time as the Going-to-the-Sun Road dedication in 1933. It is estimated that around 400 people attended, fewer than the average number that are present at any daylight moment during July or August today. The parking lot has been expanded many times through the years. The tall mountain in the background is Little Chief (9,541 feet), with the shoulder of nearby Heavy Runner (8,016 feet) visible in the right foreground. (Author's collection.)

This is a view of the Logan Pass parking lot as it appears today from the steps of the visitor center. At peak hours in August, the lot can be full by midmorning and stay that way all day. The Canadian flag is flown along with that of the United States to celebrate the honorary union of Glacier National Park with the contiguous Waterton National Park in Canada into the Waterton-Glacier International Peace Park in 1932. In an informal count of license plates lasting half a century, those from the province of Alberta usually come out somewhere in the top half dozen, along with Montana, Idaho, Washington, California, and Minnesota. (Photograph by the author.)

Pres. Franklin Delano Roosevelt was the first, and to date, the only, sitting American president to cross Glacier National Park on the Going-to-the-Sun Road. Reaching the East Side at the end of his August 5, 1934, drive, Roosevelt met with Chief Bird Rattler of the Blackfeet. (Courtesy Franklin D. Roosevelt Library.)

The Going-to-the-Sun Road can be seen crossing Haystack Butte in the background of this photograph of a young mountain goat near Logan Pass. Mountain goats, which served as the logo for the Great Northern Railway and appeared on all its Glacier National Park travel literature, are common in Glacier's high country. (Photograph by the author.)

This recently born mountain goat kid is pictured near the Hidden Lake Trail above Logan Pass. Usually born in May or June, kids weigh less than 10 pounds but are running and climbing within hours. (Photograph by the author.)

A mountain goat wanders through the Logan Pass parking lot toward the end of the day as most visitors have moved on. It is not uncommon to see multiple groups of mountain goats at or near Logan Pass. (Photograph by the author.)

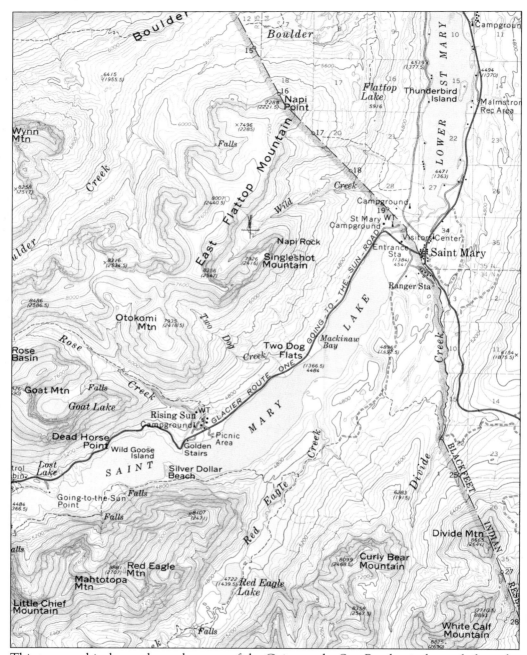

This topographical map shows the route of the Going-to-the-Sun Road as it descends from the mountains and follows the north shore of St. Mary Lake to its terminus at US Highway 89 in the small town of St. Mary. (Courtesy US Geological Survey.)

Seven

ACROSS LOGAN PASS
TO THE EAST SIDE

After crossing the Continental Divide at Logan Pass, the Going-to-the-Sun Road descends into the broad valley that leads down to St. Mary Lake. As on the West Side, the view is one of great sweeping vistas but with differences. The dominant impression here is of the vast crimson mountainsides of red Grinnell argillite, a stone which is occasionally seen on the West Side, but one from which the whole East Side seems to have been constructed.

There is another dramatic visual contrast between west and east. Beyond the western boundary of Glacier National Park, the terrain continues through heavily wooded miles and mountains across three states. On the East Side, when the Going-to-the-Sun Road ends at the edge of the park, the mountains have abruptly ended, and the Great Plains have begun.

St. Mary Lake, the second largest in the park, is 9.9 miles long, almost the same length as Lake McDonald, but narrower. It has an area of 3,923 acres, compared to McDonald's 6,823 acres. St. Mary Lake lies at an elevation of 4,484 feet, which is 1,331 feet higher than Lake McDonald on the West Side. From Logan Pass to the lake, the road quickly descends 2,162 feet in about seven miles, compared to a climb of 3,493 feet in 20 miles from Lake McDonald to the pass.

There are various tales concerning who it was who named St. Mary Lake, which was called Bow Lake by the Blackfeet. Some sources say that it was the Hudson Bay Company trader Hugh Monroe, who came to the area in the early 19th century. He lived for many years among the Blackfeet, who named him "Rising Wolf." Other stories credit the Belgian Jesuit missionary, Pierre Jean DeSmet, who spent many years in Western Montana. He visited St. Mary Lake in 1846 after crossing the Continental Divide inside present Glacier National Park.

If DeSmet did not name the lake, at least he left us an apt description of the view from its shore: "The famous [Egyptian Pyramids] Cheops and Cephren dwindle into insignificance before these gigantic peaks. The natural pyramids of the Rocky Mountains seem to hurl defiance at all human construction."

Dwarfed by the Big Drift, a bulldozer pioneers the first cut across this vast snowbank. The Big Drift is always the climax of the annual opening of the Going-to-the-Sun Road. Here, the challenges are the greatest, and the snow is the deepest. (Courtesy National Park Service.)

This view looks eastward across the Big Drift toward Piegan Mountain (9,220 feet) with Going-to-the-Sun Mountain (9,642 feet) beyond. Weather conditions and wind direction conspire to produce deeper snowbanks just east of the Continental Divide than at any other place along the Going-to-the-Sun Road. The snow can be as deep as 80 to 100 feet. (Courtesy National Park Service.)

A shovel begins the laborious task of removing snow from a cut that will eventually reach the Going-to-the-Sun Road, now buried many dozens of feet beneath. (Courtesy National Park Service.)

This view of the same shovel, looking straight down, shows that working on the Big Drift is not for the faint of heart. (Courtesy National Park Service.)

Even after the Going-to-the-Sun Road finally opens, the immense scale of the Big Drift is still explicitly evident. By August, it will be just a pair of snowbanks on a narrow section of road, but in September, the first snowfall will come, and the whole process begins all over. (Photograph by the author.)

This is the view looking eastward past the Big Drift toward Going-to-the-Sun Mountain. The line of the Going-to-the-Sun Road as it crosses the face of Piegan Mountain can be seen in the foreground. It is common for clouds to gather around the summit of Going-to-the-Sun Mountain in the afternoon. (Courtesy US Department of the Interior.)

This is a classic view of Logan Pass, presided over prominently by Clements Mountain (8,760 feet), looking westward from about four miles down the Going-to-the-Sun Road on the East Side. The line of the road can be seen on the right as it disappears into the East Side Tunnel. Following this line to the left toward Logan Pass, the remnants of the Big Drift are visible. (Photograph by the author.)

Winter is especially severe on the East Side of Glacier National Park. This photograph dramatically illustrates the effects of high wind and drifting snow on the trees that parallel the Going-to-the-Sun Road. Piegan Mountain is seen in the distance. (Courtesy National Park Service.)

This photograph provides a good view of the 405-foot East Side Tunnel, cut through the shoulder of Piegan Mountain at Mile 33.8. Much of the early excavation was by hand because power equipment could not reach it. Reminiscing about those who built the tunnel, Bill Dakin writes, "A foot trail, which you can still see, was cut high above the road. Cases of dynamite, compressors, drill steel and tools were all hand-carried on that trail, then down 100-foot ladders. Imagine going down a 100-foot ladder with 50 pounds of dynamite on your back, then back up. They weren't slackers." He also tells the story of hauling a house across Logan Pass from Lake McDonald, a project that went well—even in the West Side Tunnel and on the precarious turns of the Garden Wall—until his crew reached the East Side Tunnel. The tunnel openings had been measured, but nobody realized that the roof is concave, lower in the center than at either end. They managed to back the truck out, but it was several days before carpenters could get here to remove the peak of the roof. (Courtesy US Department of the Interior.)

In 1933, at the time of the Going-to-the-Sun Road dedication, George Alexander Grant took this photograph of the East Side Tunnel and the road. The entire length of the Going-to-the-Sun Road was not finally paved until 1952. (Courtesy National Park Service.)

Here, a line of traffic is backed up at the East Side Tunnel due to road construction. Many of the briefly stranded travelers are taking advantage of the nice weather and wonderful views of Logan Pass, surrounded by mountains, such as Clements, Reynolds, and Heavy Runner, and by other picturesque peaks and valleys. (Photograph by the author.)

The Lunch Creek Culvert is located at Mile 33.4 between the Big Drift and the East Side Tunnel. (David Restivo, National Park Service.)

Western Federal Lands Highway Program pavers work on the Going-to-the-Sun Road near Lunch Creek, with Clements Mountain in the distance. (Courtesy US Department of Transportation.)

This interpretive information sign, typical of those used in the late 20th century, overlooks the place where the Going-to-the-Sun Road rounds the Siyeh Bend and crosses Siyeh Creek at Mile 35.5. High in the background in the distance is Piegan Pass, reachable only by trail. (Courtesy US Department of the Interior.)

Dippers, or water ouzels, are unique among perching birds for their ability to swim and dive underwater. They are often seen in the streams on the East Side of Glacier National Park, such as Baring Creek, often within a short walk of the Going-to-the-Sun Road. These are pictured at Siyeh Creek. They are fascinating and enjoyable to watch as they dive, swim underwater with the current, emerge, fly upstream, and go again. (Photographs by the author.)

Jackson Glacier measures 250 acres and is the seventh largest in Glacier National Park. It is also visible from the Going-to-the-Sun Road. (Photograph by the author.)

The Jackson Glacier Overlook, located at Mile 37.3 on the Going-to-the-Sun Road, is a popular stop for motorists, most of whom will not have a better opportunity to see a glacier in the park unless they pocket their car keys and go for a hike. (Courtesy National Park Service.)

Perched on a rock atop St. Mary Falls, outdoorsman Todd Siemers points in the direction of the Going-to-the-Sun Road. The trail to St. Mary and Virginia Falls begins near the Jackson Glacier Overlook and offers an enjoyable and rewarding hike. (Photograph by the author.)

This c. 1939 view shows travelers posing on a guardrail next to a gravel Going-to-the-Sun Road. The approaching Red Bus was probably also posed. The backside (reverse of what is visible from Logan Pass) is seen in the background. (Author's collection.)

The Baring Creek Bridge at Mile 40 on the Going-to-the-Sun Road was built in 1931 by A.G. Guthrie, who built it as part of a 4.5-mile contract between Going-to-the-Sun Mountain and Dead Horse Point on St. Mary Lake. The 190-foot bridge has a 20-foot roadway and a 72-foot arch spanning the creek. (Courtesy US Department of the Interior.)

Sunrift Gorge is located on a short trail leading upstream on Baring Creek from the Going-to-the-Sun Road. (Photograph by the author.)

This is a detail of A.G. Guthrie's Baring Creek Bridge. (Historic American Engineering Record, drawn by Jessica Gibson-Withers and Albert Debnam.)

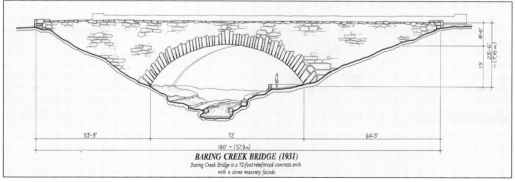

BARING CREEK BRIDGE (1931)
Baring Creek Bridge is a 72-foot reinforced concrete arch
with a stone masonry facade.

For three decades, from 1912 to the eve of World War II, the Great Northern Railway's Going-to-the-Sun Chalets were literally the crossroads of the entire East Side, and indeed, for most of Glacier National Park. They were a nexus of the vast network of trails that extended to the north and south and across the trail passes such as Gunsight Pass, which led directly to the Lake McDonald Lodge. These were served by the Bar-X-Six saddle horse concessionaire, which operated more than 1,000 head of horses and gave guided tours across the Glacier backcountry. From modest beginnings as an open camping area known as Sun Camp, the complex grew into a series of buildings that could comfortably accommodate more than 300 guests. Before the Going-to-the-Sun Road, people arrived by horseback or by boat from St. Mary. Ironically, it was the road and the rise of motor tourism that doomed the Going-to-the-Sun Chalets. People no longer wished to linger here but to drive the fascinating road. The whole chalet complex was torn down in 1948. (Author's collection.)

A tour boat makes its way across an unusually placid St. Mary Lake. Note Wild Goose Island in the distance. The Glacier Park Boat Company has long operated historic motor launches on several of Glacier's lakes. The *Little Chief* (1929) and *Joy II* (1984) operate on St. Mary Lake, while the *DeSmet* (1929) sails on Lake McDonald. (Photograph by the author.)

Triple Divide Peak (8,020 feet) is a geologic feature unique to Glacier National Park and is unique in all of North America. It is located at the intersection of the Continental Divide and the Hudson Bay Divide, meaning that it is the only point on the continent from which water flows into three oceans, the Atlantic, Pacific and Arctic. The drainage on the West Side of the park is into the Pacific; in the southern part of the park it is to the Atlantic. Crossing Logan Pass and down into the St. Mary Lake drainage, there is a small triangle of the contiguous United States where water drains to the Arctic. (Yenne family collection.)

This famous interpretive sign, adjacent to the Going-to-the-Sun Road at Mile 46.5, points out distant Triple Divide Peak and explains its great geographical significance. This location is the only place where the peak is visible from any road within the park. (Photographs by the author.)

Triple Divide Peak

Aerial view of Triple Divide Peak, looking north

Triple Divide Peak

From this viewpoint, Triple Divide is just one of many peaks. But summit hikers experience a vast alpine world: a 360-degree panorama of glaciated peaks and wilderness valleys.

Triple Divide Peak is more than a two-ocean Continental Divide. From its three-sided pyramid, rain and snowmelt travel to three major river systems and enter the Pacific Ocean, Hudson Bay, and the Gulf of Mexico.

Triple Divide Peak

Aerial photo of Triple Divide Peak, with drainages

This photograph, looking into Glacier National Park from its East Entrance, shows the old, 1940s rustic entrance station. This checking station, as they were called in early days, was demolished and replaced in 1967 by a Mission 66–style station, located about a quarter mile deeper into the park. The photographer is standing atop the bridge over Divide Creek, which marks the park boundary (8,007 feet). (Author's collection.)

The bridge across the St. Mary River at the outflow from St. Mary Lake is located at Mile 50.1, six-tenths of a mile from Divide Creek and the east entrance to Glacier National Park. It is a three-span, limestone-clad, reinforced concrete structure completed in 1935 by the Lawler Corporation to replace a one-lane steel truss bridge. (Photograph by the author.)

As seen in the 21st east entrance sign, the National Park Service has abandoned years of using uniform "1970s modern" signage to go back to a more rustic look, not unlike that seen in the postwar style on the opposite page. In the background is Singleshot Mountain (7,926 feet), with part of Flattop on the right. (David Restivo, National Park Service.)

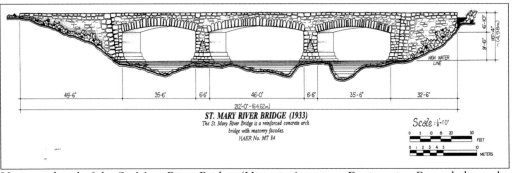

Here is a detail of the St. Mary River Bridge. (Historic American Engineering Record, drawn by Jessica Gibson-Withers and Albert Debnam.)

Pictured is the eastern end of the Going-to-the-Sun Road at St. Mary, 51 miles from the Middle Fork Bridge at West Glacier. Its intersection with US Highway 89 is a few feet to the left, and Divide Creek is three-tenths of a mile to the right. The buildings are all part of the St. Mary Lodge & Resort complex, which evolved from Hugh Black's original St. Mary Café. The gasoline prices clearly date this photograph to a bygone era. Divide Mountain (8,665 feet), which sits atop the Hudson Bay Divide, is prominent in the background. (Photograph by the author.)

Divide Creek, at Mile 50.7, marks the eastern edge of Glacier National Park, and runs parallel to the St. Mary River, which is six-tenths of a mile to the left. The Going-to-the-Sun Road crosses here and ends three-tenths of a mile to the right (see above). Almost a miniature of the St. Mary River Bridge, it was also built by Lawler and opened in 1935. The middle span is 20 feet, and the side spans are each 16 feet. The broad, rocky flood plain is evidence of the Great Flood of 1964. (Courtesy US Department of the Interior.)

Hugh and Margaret Black first opened their small gas station–restaurant–general store operation in St. Mary in 1932. By the 1950s, they had added cabins and a motel and had gradually expanded, which is seen here in 1979. Much larger lodge buildings were added around the turn of the century. After years of independent owners, the complex was acquired in 2011 by Glacier Park, Inc., which owns the other hostelries throughout the park. (Photograph by the author.)

A National Park Service vehicle is seen here parked on the approach to the Divide Creek Bridge with Singleshot Mountain overlooking St. Mary. James Willard Schultz gave it that name when he was hunting in the area with George Bird Grinnell; Grinnell bagged a running bighorn sheep with a single shot. (Photograph by the author.)

Dignitaries who gathered at Lake McDonald Hotel on June 27, 2008, at the occasion of the 75th anniversary of the Going-to-the-Sun Road, include, from left to right, James Steele Jr., chair of the Salish-Kootenai Tribes; Montana governor Brian Schweitzer; Chief Earl Old Person of the Blackfeet; Chas Cartwright, superintendent of Glacier National Park; and Bill Dakin at the podium. Both of Montana's US senators, Max Baucus and John Tester, also attended. (Courtesy Bill Dakin.)

Eight

MILESTONES

Bill Dakin was a speaker at the 50th anniversary of the Going-to-the-Sun Road in 1983, and he was a speaker again at the 75th anniversary in 2008. The following is an excerpt of his remarks at the 75th anniversary:

The road they celebrated on that day was far different than the one we know. From the West Side, people had been driving to Logan Pass since 1928. It was gravel. The lower sections from here to Logan Creek had been built cheaply, with wooden bridges and trestles. After the West Side completion in 1928, there was a pause. The Roaring Twenties imploded in 1929. The 1929 fire was a local calamity. In 1930, Highway 2 over Marias Pass was finished, which reduced urgency. But by 1932, it was done, and the first car drove over the dusty narrow road, an engineering marvel and a model for all park roads to come. For the next 25 years, interrupted only by World War II, the road was improved to what we all know it to be. I worked on the park road crew for 13 years in the 1970s and 1980s. It wasn't glamorous work. You crawled through culverts with fire hoses, cleared mud and rock slides, fixed damaged places. Some work was unpleasant. Some was exciting. The spring openings. Helping rangers with rescues. But there was never a day that I spent on the hill that I didn't appreciate that beautiful place, or failed to appreciate the heritage we bore. The history of the decisions and choices that led to the road has been written in many places. Famous men made visionary decisions. There should be a memorial to Frank Kittredge who supervised surveying it, amazingly, in 90 days in the late fall of 1924. But the stories of the not famous—the workers—are just as fascinating. Because I worked the hill, I revere the laborers who made it. There are sheltered places where the original Williams & Douglas masonry is still as pristine as when it was laid in 1926. Park your car and walk down and look at the art and craftsmanship of the Italian masons at the Baring Creek and St. Mary River Bridges. The stairs and walls George Jimm built at the Loop. Ponder the 550-foot retaining wall at the Golden Staircase. Imagine the days of the laborers who made this treasure. They were here. They built it for you. Today, we remember them and appreciate them.

The 2010 Glacier National Park Centennial festivities were attended by four former park superintendents. Flanking then superintendent Chas Cartwright (center) are, from left to right, Phil Iverson (1974–1980), David Mihalic (1994–1999), Mick Holm (2002–2008), and Bob Haraden (1980–1986). (Courtesy Bill Dakin.)

There was a sea of "flat hats" at the celebration of the Glacier National Park Centennial on May 11, 2010, in Park Headquarters. (Courtesy National Park Service.)

Steve Lozar, the secretary for the Confederated Salish and Kootenai Tribes, spoke at the Glacier National Park Centennial celebration. (Courtesy National Park Service.)

When Glacier National Park marked its 100-year milestone, chairman Willie Sharp represented the Blackfeet, who have lived on the East Side in the shadow of Glacier's mountains for centuries. (Courtesy National Park Service.)

DISCOVER THOUSANDS OF LOCAL HISTORY BOOKS
FEATURING MILLIONS OF VINTAGE IMAGES

Arcadia Publishing, the leading local history publisher in the United States, is committed to making history accessible and meaningful through publishing books that celebrate and preserve the heritage of America's people and places.

Find more books like this at
www.arcadiapublishing.com

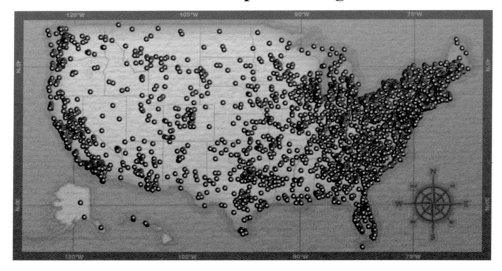

Search for your hometown history, your old stomping grounds, and even your favorite sports team.

Consistent with our mission to preserve history on a local level, this book was printed in South Carolina on American-made paper and manufactured entirely in the United States. Products carrying the accredited Forest Stewardship Council (FSC) label are printed on 100 percent FSC-certified paper.

MADE IN THE USA